P9-CJE-562

To my Dearest Friend Mary.
A friendship of more than
fifty years.
 In memory of our trip
 to the Holy Land.
     With Love
     Clarice
            December 25, 1977

THE
WALLS OF
JERUSALEM

THE WALLS OF JERUSALEM

Photography
NICOLAI CANETTI

Commentary
SANDY LESBERG

A HADDINGTON HOUSE BOOK
Distributed by THE BOBBS-MERRILL CO., INC.

FIRST PUBLISHED 1976 BY
PEEBLES PRESS INTERNATIONAL
12 Thayer St., London W1M 5LD
10 Columbus Circle, New York, N.Y. 10019

Designed by Nicolai Canetti

© Peebles Press International (Europe) Ltd
ISBN 0-672-52261-6
Library of Congress Catalog No. 76-10526

All rights reserved. No part of this book may be reproduced
in any form or by any means, except for the inclusion
of brief quotations in a review, without permission in writing from the publisher.

The publishers wish to acknowledge with great gratitude
the splendid assistance and co-operation they have received
in the preparation of this book from the Israel Government Tourist Board.

Distributed by
The Bobbs-Merrill Co. Inc.
4300 West 62nd St., Indianapolis, Indiana 46268, U.S.A.
in the United States and Canada

Meulenhoff-Bruna B.V.
Beulingstraat 2, Amsterdam, Netherlands
in the Netherlands

Printed and bound in the U.K. by
Redwood Burn Limited, Trowbridge and Esher

Jerusalem is the most personal city in the world. Her great fascination stems equally from the rich heritage of the past as well as the vitality of what she stands for today, and even though her name means peace, battle and bloodshed have been much a part of her 3,000-year history. She stands as the most important center of the three great religions of the world, yet in the name of those religions, unparalleled violence has been perpetrated by those who have insisted that devotion to the one Creator has but a single avenue – their own. And each of them has held that in His name, Jerusalem must be captured in war in order to continue its role as the city of peace. Today is no different and there are those who would fight for possession in order to change the stewardship. It is a fact that under Israeli administration all holy places, be they Jewish, Moslem or Christian, are maintained with equal care under the supervision of each religion, and free access is provided to any who wish to visit. For the first time in modern history freedom of worship is now a vital working element of daily life in Jerusalem; in sharp contrast to the immediately preceding period when Jordan held Jerusalem, and most of the Jewish places of worship were completely destroyed while Christians were denied free and regular access to their own holy places.

So if wisdom is a part of maturity, there is now the beginning of a semblance of ordered restraint in Jerusalem. After 3,000 years the City of David should be allowed to live in peace. Being the holy city of the three monotheistic faiths, she is the embodiment of much that is unique to each and yet somehow binding between all three. The Western Wall (the Wailing Wall), the most sacred Jewish site in Israel, has never been without a worshiper or pilgrim at any hour of the day or night since June 1967. It is the only relic of the great temple built by Herod in 37–34 B.C. and alone survived destruction by the Romans in 70 A.D. The Temple Mount, under Moslem control, is an enclosure within the old walled city. From it rises the Mosque of Omar, golden and glittering, that houses the rock of the Dome that is biblically acknowledged as the place where the faith of Abraham was tested by God when he was ordered to sacrifice his son Isaac. It is also thought that Mohammed ascended to heaven on his white horse from this very same spot. Deep within the old city is the Via Dolorosa in which the Ecce Homo convent stands on top of the Roman fortress where the judgement of Jesus took place. Here the Stations of the Cross leading to the Holy Sepulcher can be followed, the entire route along which Jesus carried his cross, exactly as it was nearly 2,000 years ago. It is quite clear that each person, in his own way, has very real roots in this ancient, indestructible place that has apparently been chosen by divine will to be the religious center of the world.

The narrow, shaded streets of the old city, pulsating with the same vitality as in any busy casbah in the Mediterranean world, show many diverse faces, each of them more fascinating than the next. Open-fronted markets and shops abound. Some are full of daily needs such as bread, fruit and fish, while others are bursting with exotic ancient artifacts and paraphernalia, some authentically antique, most modern replica. But it is the people that are the real wonders of the place. Arab peddlers brush by bearded rabbis, while young Israelis mingle with very old Armenian priests. Earnest, subdued nuns wend their way past old Arab coffee houses where local inhabitants sit and draw smoke from their ancient water pipes. The scent of spices fills the air, blending with the somewhat more difficult aroma that emanates from the small donkeys that can be seen careering down the cobblestone streets with sacks of coffee beans or produce swinging from their flanks. They all contribute to the unique life flow of the old city.

Outside the walls, tradition lingers immutably as a testament to the glories of the past as written in the Bible. Imagine, the tomb of David, standing near the room where the Last Supper took place. Farther away is Yad Va'shem, the eloquent memorial to the victims of the European holocaust. Also the Knesset, Israel's modern parliament building. The new city of Jerusalem is being planned carefully to maintain the architectural integrity of the adjacent antiquities and yet is as modern and up-to-date as any newly laid out city in the Western World. Of greatest importance is the fact that all the planning for the future of Jerusalem as an international center in the most real sense is *long-term*. Everything is being conceived with the idea that at last the City of David will fulfill its destiny as the great religious fount of the world. No more destruction, no more wars. Jerusalem will now be a place of peace for all people.

A painter's impression of the walls with the Citadel in the background

OPPOSITE PAGE: The Citadel (often inaccurately referred to as "David's Tower")

PRECEDING PAGE: View of the Old City from
the top of Damascus Gate walls
BELOW: View of the Northern Wall

Picturesque entrance adjacent to David's Tower

ABOVE: The Damascus Gate entrance
BELOW: View of the Wall with Citadel

OPPOSITE PAGE: Jaffa Gate, the main western thoroughfare

An Orthodox Jew walking towards Jaffa Gate

OPPOSITE PAGE: View of the Old City from above

View of gardens in front of the Northern Walls

An oriental Jewish Bar Mitzvah ceremony at the Western Wall

OPPOSITE PAGE: Revealing the Torah at the Bar Mitzvah ceremony

An Orthodox Jew praying at the Western Wall

OPPOSITE PAGE : The Western Wall, once part of the retaining
wall bordering the outer court of Herod's Temple

The Western Wall Square

The Dome of the Rock as viewed from the Mount of Olives

OPPOSITE PAGE: The golden Dome of the Rock (also called
the Mosque of Omar, named after Caliph Omar)

The Dome of the Rock

Two Arab women who do not like to be photographed . . .

. . . only from the back

PRECEDING PAGES: Views of the silver-domed Mosque of El Aksa,
Islam's holiest shrine after Mecca and Medina in Saudi Arabia

Rooftop contours in the Old City

Excavations of the Western Wall, ABOVE, and the Southern Wall, BELOW

Donkeys are very useful means of transportation
in the narrow streets of the Old City

Other useful means of transportation are heads . . .

Children playing through the streets of the Old City . . .

Sitting is also a favorite occupation in the streets

Two Israeli soldiers and two Arabs shopping in the Old City

PRECEDING PAGE: View of city from the Mount of Olives

It is typical to see priests from all corners of the world

The square outside the Church of the Holy Sepulchre

Via Dolorosa, the Way of the Cross

An Armenian convent in the Old City

A completely veiled woman

Greek priests

A religious consultation

PRECES SVPPLICATIONESQVE CVM CLAMORE VALIDO ET LACRYMIS OFFERENS EXAVDITVS EST PRO SVA REVERENTIA

View of the Mount of Olives with the Church of All Nations
in the foreground

The Russian church on the Mount of Olives

The Mount of Olives as seen through the graceful arches
on the Temple Mount

The rock-hewn tomb of Zacharias, father of John the Baptist

OVERLEAF: The impressive Dormition Abbey on Mount Zion